PACIFIC PARK

3.0

Artistic Adventures

PUPPETS

Kelly Burkholder

The Rourke Press, Inc.
Vero Beach, Florida 32964

PHOTO CREDITS
© Rick Lyon: cover, pages 19, 21; © Looking Glass Production: pages 4, 17;
© Bonnie Periace page 7; © East Coast Studios: pages 8, 9, 11, 12, 13, 16;
© Puppetworks: pages 15 (T.A. Smith), 22 (Larry Rush)

PRODUCED & DESIGNED by East Coast Studios
eastcoaststudios.com

EDITORIAL SERVICES:
Pamela Schroeder

Library of Congress Cataloging-in-Publication Data

Burkholder, Kelly, 1970-
    Puppets / Kelly Burkholder.
        p. cm. — (Artistic adventures)
    Includes bibliographical references and index.
    Summary: Discusses the history and use of puppets, different kinds of puppets and how to make them, and
putting on a puppet show.
    ISBN 1-57103-355-6
    1. Puppets—Juvenile literature. 2. Puppet making—Juvenile literature. 3. Puppet theater—Juvenile literature.
[1. Puppets. 2. Puppet making.] I. Title.

PN1972 .B84 2000
791.5'3—dc21
                                                                00–025372

Printed in the USA

Contents

Where Puppets Came From

Puppets have been around for a long time. Some of the first puppets were really masks. People wore these masks over their faces. Have you ever worn a mask?

Later puppets began to look like dolls. These dolls had arms and legs that a **puppeteer** (PUP ih TEER) moved. Churches used puppets to teach people. Monks and priests were the puppeteers. Then people used puppets to make people laugh. Puppets were very popular in carnivals and fairs. Long ago, puppet shows were as popular in Europe as movies are today.

Sometimes puppets are used as characters in plays.

Use of Puppets

The puppeteer brings a puppet to life. He or she makes the audience believe in the puppet **character** (KAYR ik ter). Have you ever watched Sesame Street? The characters like Big Bird, Elmo, and the Cookie Monster are puppets. Which is your favorite character? Puppets help you make people laugh and learn. In a puppet show you can pretend to be somebody else. It's a great place to tell stories.

The puppeteer is hidden below the table where the audience and T.V. cameras cannot see him.

Making Puppets

You can turn almost anything into puppets: socks, mittens, paper bags, and more. Look around your house. All you need is a scrap of cloth or paper. Don't forget **creativity** (KREE ay TIV ih tee).

This family is making puppets out of things they found in their home.

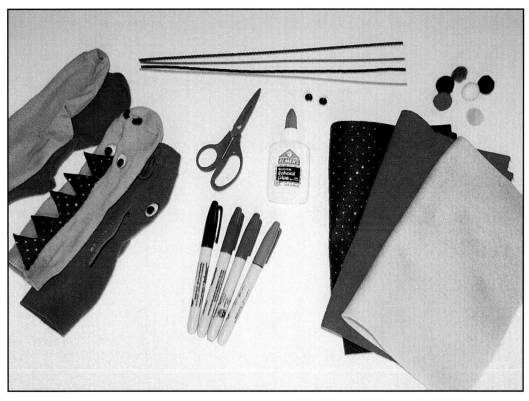

All types of things can be used to make puppets.

You can give your puppet long hair using yarn or big eyes using buttons. How about a long tongue? Use a piece of ribbon or felt to make a tongue. Let your imagination run wild. When you get started you will see how easy it is to make puppets.

Types of Puppets

There are many kinds of puppets. Sock puppets, finger puppets, paper bag puppets, hand puppets, **marionettes** (MAYR ee eh NETS), and **ventriloquist** (ven TRIL eh kwist) puppets are just a few.

To make a sock puppet, use an old sock. Put the sock over your hand. Move it around as if it had a mouth. You can use all kinds of things to decorate your sock puppet. Use buttons, thread, yarn, or felt to make eyes, ears, hair, or whatever you like.

Sock puppets are fun to create and play with.

Finger puppets are very easy to make. Take an old glove and cut off the finger tips. Add eyes, ears, or hair like you did with the sock puppets. Now that you have made your finger puppet, try it on for size. Slip it on your finger. Move your finger around. You can make your puppet nod his head when you bend your finger. Can you think of other ways to move your finger puppet?

You can perform a finger puppet play with just two fingers.

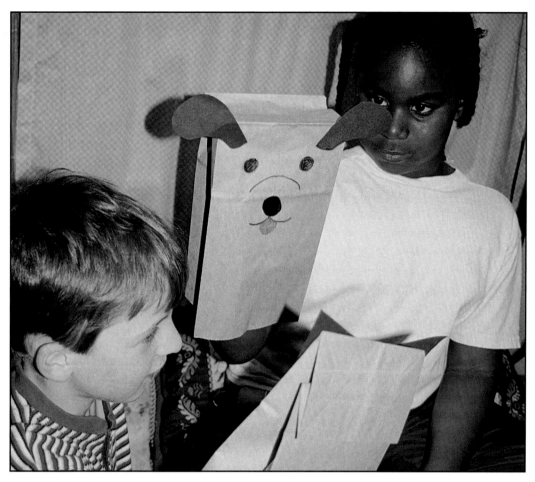

Children work together to make paper bag puppets.

Try making a paper bag puppet. It's fun to make a cat or dog puppet. Draw the face of your cat or dog on the bag. Use pipe cleaners for whiskers. Cut paper or felt ears and glue them on the bag.

A marionette is a puppet on strings like Pinnochio. The puppeteer stands over the puppet. He or she moves strings on the puppet's legs, arms, and head. Marionettes are harder to use than other puppets. However, if you practice you can have fun using a marionette.

It takes many strings and a lot of practice to use a marionette puppet.

Hand puppets are very popular. Hand puppets fit over your hand like a glove. Sometimes they are called glove puppets. Hand puppets are easy to use. You slip your hand into the puppet. Use your thumb and a finger to move the puppet's arms. Can you make the puppet clap his hands? Can you wave good-bye?

Hand puppets are easy to make and use.

This woman is able to change her voice so that it sounds like the goose is talking.

Ventriloquists have puppets sitting on their knees. A ventriloquist puppet has an open space in the back. The ventriloquist uses his or her hand to move the puppet's mouth. It looks like the puppet is really talking. Ventriloquists need to "throw" their voices. It should sound like the puppet is talking, not the ventriloquist.

Movements

Think of ways to move your puppet. How would it move if it were excited? What about angry, or scared, or sleepy? Try to make your puppet act cold. You can make him shiver when you shake your hands. You can make your puppet talk, too. Practice with your puppets before you begin a puppet show. Remember, practice makes perfect.

This puppet shows expression by moving his arms, head, and mouth.

Puppet Shows

Puppets are a great way to **entertain** (EN ter TAYN) people of all ages. Children love to learn about new things by watching puppets. Adults like watching puppet shows, too. You can find puppets in many places. They are on television. They are in your classroom. They are also in libraries. Puppets are a great way to make smiles. Do you have a favorite puppet **memory** (MEM uh REE)?

Puppets help tell stories and entertain people of all ages.

Glossary

character (KAYR ik ter) — a person in a play; the person could be an actor, a puppet, an animal, or many other things

creativity (KREE ay TIV ih tee) — being able to make something, or think of new ideas

entertain (EN ter TAYN) — to make people have a good time

marionette (MAYR ee eh NET) — a puppet moved by strings

memory (MEM uh REE) — a picture of the past that you see in your mind

puppeteer (PUP ih TEER) — someone who uses puppets in puppet shows

ventriloquist (ven TRIL eh kwist) — a person who makes it sound like his or her voice is coming from somewhere else

Marionette puppets are used to act out **The Wizard of Oz.**

Index

Further Reading

Find out more about puppets with these helpful information sites:

www.stagehandpuppets.com
www.puppetfun.com
www.amazingpuppets.com
Rick Lyon Puppets: www.lyonpuppets.com
The Puppetworks, Inc.: www. puppetworks.org